KU-213-786

FACES

Christopher McHugh

Wayland

Discovering Art

Animals
Faces
Food
People at Work
Town and Country
Water

Cover: Senecio, *a face painted in 1922 by the Swiss artist Paul Klee. Kunstmuseum, Basle, Switzerland.*

Editor: Rosemary Ashley
Designer: David Armitage
Special Consultant: Pauline Ridley, Lecturer in History of Art and Design at the University of Brighton and the Open University.

This edition published in 1994
by Wayland (Publishers) Ltd

First published in 1992 by
Wayland (Publishers) Ltd
61 Western Road, Hove
East Sussex BN3 1JD

© Copyright 1992 Wayland (Publishers) Limited

British Library Cataloguing in Publication Data
McHugh, Christopher
Faces. – (Discovering Art Series)
I. Title. II. Series
704.942

HARDBACK ISBN 0-7502-0510-5

PAPERBACK ISBN 0-7502-1337-X

Typeset by Type Study, Scarborough, England
Printed and bound in Italy by G. Canale & C.S.p.A., Turin

Contents

1 Faces in art

A face is perhaps the first thing that we recognize with our eyes. Young babies soon begin to respond to the sight of their mother's face, and later on to those of other people.

We all learn to understand what the expressions on people's faces mean; angry or sad, happy or unsure. We use our faces to show much more than we can say in words. We look at people's faces to see if they are telling the truth, or making a joke, or lying. Through thousands of years, actors have used their faces, or masks which represent faces, to help show the meaning of the play or dance which they are performing.

When you first made a picture of a face it was probably just a circle, perhaps with two dots for eyes and two lines for the nose and mouth. Try now and see if you can make a really simple drawing that is still a recognizable face. Try making a face using lots of different shapes. Look at the simple shapes Paul Klee has used to make the face in his picture, *Senecio*, shown on the cover of this book.

There are faces in just about every kind of art, made with all sorts of materials. Picture **1** shows a huge stone carving of a face made by the Olmec people, who lived 2,000 years ago in the country that is now Mexico. The carving was made by chipping away little bits of an enormous block of stone, to finally leave the shape of the head standing free.

In the following pages you will see and read about many kinds of art, showing faces from different times and from countries all over the world.

1 (opposite) *This gigantic stone figure was carved by the Olmec people, who belonged to a very early civilization living in Mexico between two and three thousand years ago. It is at La Venta in Mexico.*

2 Ancient faces

We can often see faces in art from ancient civilizations such as that of Egypt, in books, museums and films. During the thousands of years of the Ancient Egyptian civilization, many pictures and sculptures were made showing faces. But we see fewer faces made by the people who lived in Mesopotamia, the area which we now call Iraq. Their civilizations were as old as Egypt, but very little of their art remains because they did not have, many long-lasting building materials available, such as stone.

Picture **2** is a rare example of a Sumerian painting. The people of Sumer were among the earliest of those who lived in Mesopotamia. The painting dates from about 2600 BC and is rather like a cartoon in the way it shows people. See how the artist has picked out the important features to draw most clearly – noses, eyes, the shape of heads, ears, eyebrows . . .

2 *A Sumerian picture showing a musician playing a lyre to celebrate a victory in battle. The man on the left is an army officer and the woman behind is a singer. British Museum, London.*

3 *The head and shoulders of a statue of the Egyptian Princess Nofret. The statue is one of a pair – the other is of her husband Prince Rahotep. Egyptian Museum, Cairo.*

4 (below) *The gold mask of Tutankhamun, the Egyptian boy king who ruled Egypt in the thirteenth century BC. He was only eighteen when he died and was buried in Thebes in a coffin with this mask at its head. Egyptian Museum, Cairo.*

These two Egyptian heads are both sculptures. Picture **3** shows a stone sculpture of a princess called Nofret. It has been painted to pick out certain features more clearly, especially the princess' clothes and the make-up which she often used. Take a look at picture **31** on page 27. Both these pictures show a woman with make-up on. What are the differences between the two pictures?

The head of King Tutankhamun, picture **4**, is made from gold and is part of the rich coffin made for his preserved body, called a mummy. The mummy was found, with this marvellous mask and many other treasures, in a tomb inside a pyramid in Egypt.

5 *A bronze head of the Greek god Apollo. It was found in Cyprus and is now in the British Museum, London.*

6 (below) *A marble sculpture of the head of the Roman Emperor Hadrian, who ruled from AD 117–138. British Museum, London.*

Picture **5** is a sculpture from the period known as Classical Greece (around 500–300 BC). It shows the head of the god Apollo. The sculpture is made from a metal called bronze, through a process called casting. To cast an object a mould has first to be made. If you think of pressing something into clay or plasticine and then carefully removing it, that will give you an idea of how a mould can be made. Then a liquid substance is poured into the mould and allowed to set. In the case of bronze, it has to be heated until it melts, setting hard again as it cools. Pictures **11** and **15** on pages 12 and 15 also show bronze castings.

The Romans learned a great deal from the Greeks, especially about art. Picture **6** is a sculpture of the Roman Emperor Hadrian. It is much more a portrait of the actual person than the Greek god Apollo (picture **5**) or Tutankhamun's golden mask (picture **4**).

Picture **7** is a mosaic, which is a picture made by sticking small pieces of coloured stone onto a floor or wall. This mosaic comes from Cirencester in England and it shows how the Romans took their art to all parts of their enormous empire. Look how the face is shown, using simple, heavily outlined shapes, filled in with the little coloured pieces.

7 Part of a mosaic on the floor of a Roman villa in Corinium, present-day Cirencester, England. The mosaic shows the four seasons – this is of Autumn.

3 Faces in art around the world

Here are three pictures of faces made by the original peoples of North and South America (see also picture **1**). Picture **8** is a painting made by the Aztecs. Like the Olmecs, who made the stone sculpture in picture **1**, the Aztecs also lived in the area now called Mexico, but many centuries later. The painting shows the sun god (top left) and the god of darkness (below) and is actually a kind of writing in pictures. The strong outlines and clear colours make it look like a modern cartoon. If you compare this

8 *A page from an Aztec sacred book called a codex. The Aztecs lived in Mexico in the fifteenth century. Their sacred books contained 'picture writing' which could be understood by different tribes who spoke different languages. University Library, Bologna, Italy.*

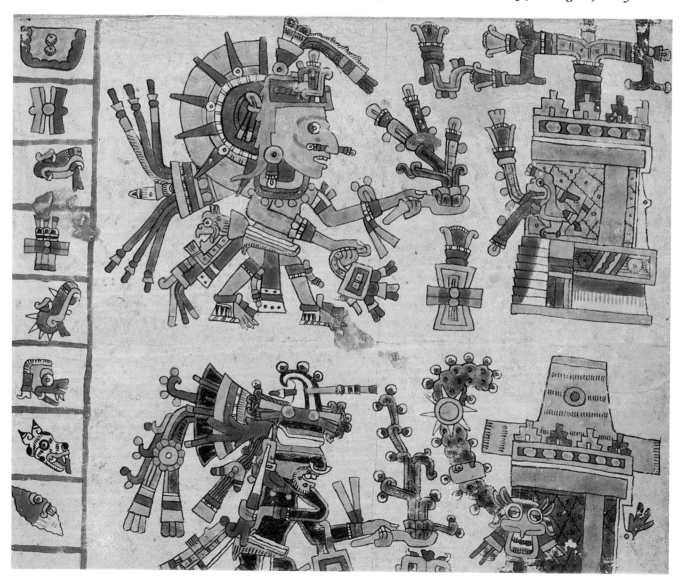

9 *The painted wooden mask of a Tsimshian girl. It has human hair, and wooden hair decorations in the shape of birds with hinged wings. Portland Art Museum, Oregon, USA.*

10 (below) *The mask of a dancer used by the Kwakiutl tribespeople living in Canada. Field Museum of National History, Chicago, USA.*

picture with picture **2** (page 6), you can see that although the clothes the gods are wearing are more important, the whole picture also makes a flat pattern.

Faces often appear in the art of the tribespeople living on the north-west coast of North America. Picture **9** is a mask of a girl from the Tsimshian tribe. It is quite life-like and uses real human hair to make it look even more real. Picture **10**, a carved wooden mask, is much less like a real person's face. It has a hooked bird beak for a nose, hands for cheeks, simple eyes, mouth and ears, and a plaited string for hair and beard. It was made by the Kwakiutl tribe and would have been used as part of the costume in special tribal dances.

The huge continent of Africa, with its many different peoples, has a very ancient history. The earliest human beings are thought to have lived in Africa. The pictures here show two of the many different ways of making faces in art that can be found in Africa.

Picture **11** (like picture **5** on page 8) is another bronze casting, made in West Africa over six hundred years ago. It is very like a real person's face. Picture **12** is very different from picture **11**. It is a wooden carving covered with a sheet of metal, which has had a pattern of dents beaten into it. It was made by the BaKota people of Gabon, in West Africa. Can you see how the face is made from very unrealistic shapes; notice the cross in which the nose and eyes appear.

11 (above) *A bronze head made by a West African sculptor about five hundred years ago. British Museum, London.*

12 *A head made from wood covered with beaten brass, made by the BaKota people in West Africa. Entwistle Gallery, London.*

The carved wooden Maori mask from New Zealand, picture **13**, is covered with a pattern of tattoos, in circles, coils and parallel lines. Can you see how the patterns are a little like the unrealistic shapes of the face in picture **12**? The shapes and patterns in pictures like **12** and **13** had a great influence on modern artists, for instance Picasso, Jawlensky and Klee (see pictures **29** and **30** on pages 26 and 27 and the cover picture).

This book shows several ways in which people have made sculptures of faces. The process of casting was described on page 8, and there are examples of carved wood and stone – for instance pictures **1** and **13** (pages 5 and 13). Picture **14**, like picture **12** on page 12, is an example of beaten metal work. This time the metal used is silver. The picture shows the face of a god on part of a cauldron from Northern Europe. It was made by the Celts about the year AD 1000. See how the artist has used strong, clear lines for this face, for instance in the eyebrows and sides of the moustache.

14 *The face of a Celtic god, on the side of a cauldron made from beaten silver. National Museum, Copenhagen, Denmark.*

15 *The bronze head of a Buddha made in the seventeenth century in Thailand.*

16 (below) *An ancient stone carving of a man's head, from China.*

Picture **15** is a bronze cast statue from Thailand. It shows the head of the eastern religious teacher known as the Buddha. Picture **16** shows a Chinese head that has been carved from stone. Can you see that both these sculptures express calmness and peacefulness? Gently curving shapes and lines have been used to create this calm and peaceful feeling. But look how much clearer and sharper the lines are that the Thai artist has used, for instance on the eyebrows, down the nose, around the lips and for the eyelids. The Chinese face is very much rounder, fuller and more solid.

4 Greek and Roman influences

Picture **17** shows a painting on a wooden panel. It is a portrait made to be placed on a coffin – like the golden head of Tutankhamun, picture **4**, page 7. The face was painted in Egypt about 2,000 years ago, during the time when Egypt was part of the Roman Empire. This style of painting was called Graeco-Roman because the style was invented by Greeks but later used by artists all over the Roman Empire.

Picture **18** is a mosaic made by a Christian artist living in the Byzantine Empire (present-day Greece and Turkey) at the end of the twelfth century. The mosaic is a little like picture **17** above. It shows the same long nose and heavy eyelids but this image of Jesus Christ is not at all like an image of a real person.

17 (above) A Man with a Wreath – *a portrait painted on a wooden panel, made in Egypt about the year AD 1. The National Gallery, London.*

18 *A mosaic of Jesus Christ dating from the twelfth century. It is in a church in present-day Greece.*

19 Jeanne Hébuterne *a portrait painted by the twentieth-century Italian artist Amedeo Modigliani. Christies, London.*

Picture **19** is by the twentieth century artist Amedeo Modigliani. Can you see how he has used some ideas about painting faces from the art shown in pictures **17** and **18**? Look at the long stretched shape of the face and the clear, curving outlines. This is just one example of the influence of Classical Greece and Rome on art of later times.

5 The Renaissance

20 Mona Lisa *by Leonardo da Vinci – the world's most famous portrait. The Louvre, Paris.*

The period known as the Renaissance began in Italy in about the fifteenth century. It was a time when earlier Greek and Roman ideas were rediscovered and became popular. Two of the greatest artists of this time and two of the best-known of any time, are the Italians Leonardo da Vinci and Michelangelo. Both men were fascinated by people and by faces.

Picture **20** shows one of the most famous paintings of a face in the world. It is *Mona Lisa* by Leonardo. It is a portrait of a mysterious woman in front of a background of countryside. People often ask why is the picture so famous, and why is *Mona Lisa* just beginning to smile? Many people have tried to answer these two questions, but no one can agree who is right.

Michelangelo was a very famous sculptor as well as a great painter. One of his best-known works is the huge painting he made to cover the ceiling of the Sistine Chapel in the Vatican in Rome. Picture **21** is a small section of this painting, showing the Bible story of God separating the land from the seas as He creates the world. God is shown as an old man, with fluffy beard and hair and wrinkly skin, a rather different image than that of Jesus Christ in picture **18** on page 16. Michelangelo's painting is a fresco, which means it is painted straight on to a plaster wall (or ceiling) and becomes part of the surface of the wall itself.

21 *A detail from the painting of the creation of the world by Michelangelo, on the ceiling of the Sistine Chapel in the Vatican in Rome.*

The ideas of the Renaissance started in Italy and gradually spread throughout Europe. They were soon taken up in the Netherlands, in the region that is now Belgium. Picture **22** is by one of the earliest of the great painters of the Netherlands, Rogier van der Weyden. Although most of the pictures painted at this time were still of subjects concerned with the Christian religion, van der Weyden was beginning, like other artists, to paint portraits of real people. Picture **22** shows a woman of the period as she actually looked. See how her eyes sparkle.

22 Portrait of a Woman *painted by Rogier van der Weyden in the Netherlands at the beginning of the Renaissance period. Staatliche Gemäldegalerie, Berlin, Germany.*

23 *A self-portrait by Rembrandt van Rijn, one of many that he made to mark the stages of his life. Kenwood House, London.*

Rembrandt's portrait of himself (picture **23**) is also from the Netherlands, but it is from Holland which is further north, and painted about two hundred years later. It was made not to sell but as a record of the artist's own appearance. Like picture **22**, it is also an oil painting, but Rembrandt has used the paint in a different way to van der Weyden. Can you see how differently? Look at how the two artists have shown the edges of things, and how they have shown light and shadow. Rembrandt painted many self-portraits and they form a special set of paintings, sometimes thought to be his greatest work, recording how he changed through the years of his long life.

6 Weird faces

Until the invention of photography in the mid-nineteenth century, many forms of art needed to show people's faces as they actually looked. But this has not been the only reason why artists have liked to show faces. Many have used faces in their art to express their feelings about people or the world in which they live.

The three paintings of these pages deliberately show strange faces. Hieronymus Bosch was an artist with strong religious beliefs. He lived at the time of the Reformation, when great changes were taking place in the Christian Church. In his painting (picture **24**) showing Jesus Christ before his crucifixion, he shows the cruelty and wickedness which causes such suffering.

24 Christ crowned with thorns *by Hieronymus Bosch. The National Gallery, London.*

Bosch has painted the people's clothes and their tools to show this cruelty, but even more importantly, he has shown the evil character and behaviour of those who tortured Christ in the ugliness and cruelty of their faces.

Giuseppe Arcimboldo's strange picture of a face made out of fruit and vegetables (picture **25**) is typical of many of his paintings. It is a way of showing a fantastic view of familiar things. The painting is meant to surprise and amuse those who look at it.

25 Whimsical Portrait *A strange picture of fruit, nuts and vegetables that form a face, by Giuseppe Arcimboldo. Nostell Priory, Yorkshire, England.*

26 Old Women *by Francisco de Goya. He painted these witch-like figures late in his life, when he often showed frightening images, both real and imagined. Musée des Beaux-Arts, Lille, France.*

Francisco de Goya was a Spanish artist who lived through a very difficult period in his country's history, when Spain was fighting the armies of the French Emperor Napoleon. During this time Goya saw many terrible things. In his later life he also suffered an illness which caused him to become deaf. He began to paint terrifying pictures of monsters, horrible-looking people and gruesome acts of war. Often he used faces to show the awfulness of his subjects, as in picture **26**. How has Goya made these old women look so horrible?

7 Modern faces

27 Head of a young girl, *a portrait made in pastels by Mary Cassatt. Musée de Petit Palais, Paris.*

The modern period of art is usually said to have begun in the second half of the nineteenth century. Mary Cassatt was an American artist who lived and worked in France at that time, with the group of artists who became known as the Impressionists. In picture 27 we see a portrait she made of a small child. She used a special kind of chalk, called pastel, to make this picture. Much of the picture is left only partly finished, but the face has had a lot more work done on it. Can you see where Cassatt has left areas of the paper blank, and where she has made rapid marks almost like scribbling?

Vincent van Gogh is now a very famous artist, although during his lifetime hardly anybody had heard of him. Picture **28** is a self-portrait made after he had injured himself by deliberately cutting off a piece of his ear. Van Gogh was Dutch but he spent the last years of his life as a painter in France. There he saw the work of the Impressionists and he used many of their ideas in his art. Can you see the brushmarks in this painting? They are left clearly showing in parts of the picture. These brushmarks, and the bright colours van Gogh has used, give the picture a sort of energy or sense of movement.

28 *A self-portrait painted by Vincent van Gogh after he had cut off part of his ear while feeling very upset. Courtauld Institute Galleries, London.*

Pablo Picasso was a Spanish artist who, like van Gogh, spent much time in France. Picture **29** shows the head of a woman who, the title tells us, is weeping. Can you see the handkerchief and the tears? Picasso has used heavy dark lines to draw the shapes which make up the woman's face. Would you say this picture is anything like picture **12**, on page 12, and if so, why? In this book, can you find any other pictures from earlier times which are a little like Picasso's painting?

29 Weeping Woman *by Pablo Picasso. Private collection. © DACS 1992.*

The picture on the cover of this book, called *Senecio*, is by a Swiss artist, Paul Klee. Picture **30** is by a Russian artist, Alexej von Jawlensky. Both these artists worked for a time in Germany, with other artists who called themselves The Blue Rider Group, in the early years of the twentieth century. Can you see any likenesses in their two pictures? Colours and shapes are very important in each.

In picture **30**, Jawlensky uses colours and shapes to produce a mood or feeling rather than to describe a real face. Klee's picture, on the cover, is also of an imaginary face, but with more definite edges. Like Picasso, in picture **29**, Klee shows the side view of the nose in his painting and the front view of both eyes. Can you see how each artist has done this? Now take another look at picture **2** (page 6). Can you see how the artist here has also shown a front view of the eye and a side view of the nose on each person's face?

Picture **31** is by the American artist Andy Warhol. It is a screen print showing a famous film star called Marilyn Monroe. The features of her face are drawn with the black layer and then simple, flat shapes of colour are put on to certain areas – pink skin, yellow hair, red lips, blue eyelids. The black layer of the print is taken from a photograph. The coloured areas show the make-up that Marilyn was well-known for – bright lipstick, bleached hair, heavy eye-shadow. Warhol's pictures often point out the difference between the real thing, and pictures of the real thing which we see so often in our modern world in magazines, television and films.

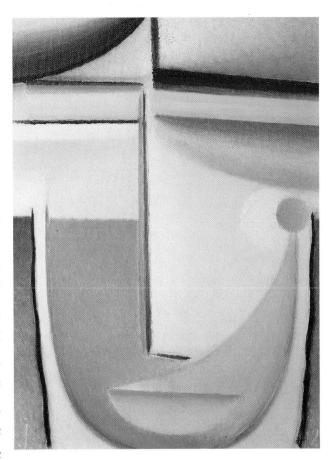

30 Symphony in Rose *by Alexej von Jawlensky, Frankfurt, Germany.*

31 Marilyn, *Andy Warhol's screen print of Marilyn Monroe, made in 1967.* © *ARS.*

Who are the artists and where are their works?

Giuseppe Arcimboldo (c.1530–93) Italian
An artist who became very famous during his lifetime for paintings of faces made up of objects such as vegetables, flowers and fruit. His work can be seen in some of the larger collections of paintings in European cities. Picture **25**, page 22.

Hieronymus Bosch (c.1450–1516) Dutch
A painter of strange and fantastic pictures, many of them expressing religious ideas. Little is known about his early life but he lived and worked in the Netherlands, in the town of 's Hertogenbosch, from which his name is taken. Bosch's work can be seen in important collections all over the world, including the Louvre in Paris, the National Gallery, London, and the Metropolitan Museum, New York. Picture **24**, page 22.

Mary Cassatt (1845–1926) American
An Impressionist painter whose favourite subjects were women and children. She was greatly influenced by Japanese prints. Her work can be seen in many important American collections such as in Baltimore, Philadelphia and New York, and also in major European galleries. Picture **27**, page 24.

Vincent van Gogh (1853–90) Dutch
He was born in the Netherlands but painted many of his best-known pictures in France. He was influenced by the work of Dutch painters of the past, by the clear, bright colours of Japanese prints, and most importantly, by the Impressionist painters. Like the Impressionists, van Gogh painted pictures of people and things around him. His work can be seen in important collections all over the world, and especially in the Musée d'Orsay in Paris and Van Gogh Museum in Amsterdam; also in the National, Tate and Courtauld Institute Galleries in London. Picture **28**, page 25.

Francisco de Goya (1746–1828) Spanish
He became a successful court painter, painting many portraits of the royal family and other important people, but he often showed unfavourable sides of their characters. In 1808 the French invaded Spain and Goya worked on a series of famous prints called *The Disasters of War*, which showed the cruelty and horror of war. His work can be seen in major collections all over the world, especially in the Prado in Madrid, at the National and Courtauld Institute Galleries in London, and the National Gallery and Phillips Collection in Washington. Picture **26**, page 23.

Alexej von Jawlensky (1864–1941) Russian
A painter who, after spending some time in the Russian army, studied and worked in Germany from about 1896. In his later life he formed a group called the Blue Four, with three other well-known painters, including Paul Klee. His work can be seen in certain major collections, especially in Pasadena, USA and Wiesbaden, Germany. Picture **30**, page 27.

Paul Klee (1879–1940) Swiss
A printmaker and painter who studied and worked in Switzerland and Germany. His travels in North Africa influenced his feeling for colour. Klee was connected to the 'Blue Rider' and 'Blue Four' groups of painters in Germany, along with Alexej von Jawlensky. His work can be seen in collections of modern art throughout the world and especially at the Klee Foundation, Berne, Switzerland. Cover picture.

Leonardo da Vinci (1452–1519) Italian
A brilliant artist, scientist and inventor who lived during the Renaissance. He is one of the most famous of all European artists. The *Mona Lisa* is probably Leonardo's most famous work. Few of his paintings and inventions were completed, but the huge quantity of notes and drawings which he left behind are among the greatest works of the Renaissance. Major works can be seen in Italy, and in Paris, Washington, and the National Gallery in London. The best collection of Leonardo's drawings is in the Royal Library at Windsor Castle, near London. Picture **20**, page 18.

Michelangelo (Buonarroti) (1475–1564)
Italian
Along with Leonardo and Raphael, he is considered to be the greatest artist of the Renaissance. Like Leonardo, Michelangelo had many talents – he is probably most famous as a sculptor, although the painting on the ceiling of the Sistine Chapel is also a world-famous work. He was also well-known as a poet. Michelangelo's works can be seen especially in Italy, and in the National Gallery, Royal Academy and British Museum in London. Picture **21**, page 19.

Amedeo Modigliani (1884–1920) Italian
A sculptor and painter who worked mainly in Paris. Modigliani was a brilliant draughtsman. He is best known for his pictures of people whose heads and features he usually elongated (made longer). His works can be seen in major collections around the world, and in the Tate Gallery, the Victoria and Albert Museum and the Courtauld Institute Galleries, London. Picture **19**, page 17.

Pablo Picasso (1881–1973) Spanish
He was born in Malaga, Spain, but after a visit to Paris in 1900, he lived permanently in France. He was one of the leading experimenters in art. With Georges Braque, he developed the style of art called Cubism. Picasso was perhaps the greatest artist of the twentieth century and produced a huge amount of work. His work can be seen in major galleries all over the world. Picture **29**, page 26.

Rembrandt (van Rijn) (1606–69) Dutch
One of the greatest of all Dutch painters. Early in his career he was a successful painter of large pictures of religious and classical stories. Later he earned his living as a portrait painter. Throughout his career he painted portraits of himself which reflected his advancing years and changing mood. Many believe them to be his finest work. His work can be seen in galleries all over the world, especially in Holland, and at the National Gallery, Kenwood House, Wallace Collection (all in London), also in Cambridge, Edinburgh, Glasgow, Liverpool, and Dublin in Eire. There is a huge collection of his drawings and etchings in his house in Amsterdam. Picture **23**, page 21.

Andy Warhol (c.1928–1987) American

An American artist associated with 'Pop Art', so called because it used popular culture such as comics, advertisements and films. Warhol especially made use of familiar products produced in their millions, such as tinned soup and newspaper photographs, often making bright coloured screen prints of them. His work can be seen in major collections of modern art all over the world. Picture **31**, page 27.

Rogier van der Weyden (c.1399–1464) Flemish

He is one of the most important Flemish painters of the fifteenth century. Van der Weyden was very successful and became City Painter in Brussels. His paintings express feelings much more than most other Flemish painters of the same period. His work can be seen in major collections around the world and in the National Gallery, London. Picture **22**, page 20.

Glossary

Bronze A type of metal, made from copper and tin and used for making tools and sculpture.

Brushmarks The marks left by a brush in a painting.

Byzantine Empire The Roman Empire in the East, founded by Emperor Constantine I, who moved from Rome to Constantinople (now Istanbul) in the fourth century AD.

Cartoon An amusing drawing making fun of something or someone.

Casting Producing a shape by pouring or pressing liquid wax, plastic, bronze or other metal into a mould.

Cauldron A large, heavy pot, used for boiling liquids.

Celts A people who settled all over western Europe, in pre-Roman times.

Civilization A stage in the development of the way people live together in groups.

Christian Someone who practises the religion based on the teachings of Jesus Christ.

Classical Relating to the Ancient Greeks and Romans.

Crucifixion The death of Jesus Christ on the cross.

Draughtsman Someone skilled in drawing.

Egyptian mummy An embalmed or preserved body that was prepared for burial in Ancient Egypt.

Fresco A way of painting straight on to newly-plastered walls or ceilings.

Graeco-Roman The period from around 100 BC to AD 100, when art was influenced by Greek and Roman styles.

Impressionists A group of artists painting towards the end of the nineteenth century in France. They used sketchy brushstrokes to record the effects of weather and light in their paintings.

Mosaic A picture or pattern made by sticking pieces of stone or glass into a floor or wall.

Mould A shape into which a melted liquid substance is poured. The substance takes on the shape of the mould as it hardens.

Oil painting A painting either on stretched canvas or wood, where the artist uses a type of paint in which the colour is held together with linseed or poppy seed oil.

Pastels Coloured, chalky crayons.

Portrait A picture of a person intended to be a record of what that person looks like.

Pyramid A triangular structure built by the Ancient Egyptians for the Tombs of their Kings.

Reformation The religious movement of the sixteenth century which resulted in the establishment of Protestant Churches.

Renaissance A time of rediscovery in Europe of ideas from Ancient Greece and Rome.

Roman Empire The territories ruled by Ancient Rome. The head of the Empire was called the Emperor.

Screen print A print made with cloth, where the ink is pressed through the weave.

Sculpture The art of carving, casting or modelling statues and designs.

Self-portrait A picture painted by the artist of him or herself.

Tattoos Designs made on the skin by pricking and staining it.

Unrealistic Not having a believable appearance.

Villa In Ancient Rome, a large country house.

Books to read

The Book of Art – A Way of Seeing (Ernest Benn, 1979).

Every Picture Tells a Story by Rolf Harris (Phaidon, 1989).

Faces – Looking at Art by Giles Waterfield (Wayland, 1983).

Families – through the eyes of artists by Wendy and Jack Richardson (Macmillan, 1990).

Great Painters by Piero Ventura (Kingfisher, 1989).

Just Look . . . A Book about Paintings by Robert Cumming (Viking Kestrel, 1986).

Painting and Sculpture by Jillian Powell (Wayland, 1989).

Penguin Dictionary of Art and Artists by Peter and Linda Murray (Penguin, 1989).

20th Century Art by Jillian Powell (Wayland, 1989).

Picture acknowledgements

The publishers have attempted to contact all copyright holders of the illustrations in this title, and apologise if there have been any oversights.

The photographs in this book were supplied by: The Ancient Art and Architecture Collection © Ronald Sheridan 7 (lower); Bridgeman Art Library cover, 17, 18, 19, 20, 22 (both), 24, 27 (both). Courtauld Institute/Bridgeman 25; Giraudon/Bridgeman 23; Kenwood House/Bridgeman 21; Michael Holford © 6, 8 (top), 9, 12 (top), 16 (lower), 26. National Gallery/C. McHugh 16 (top); Werner Forman Archive 5, 7, (top), 8 (lower), 10, 11 (both), 12 (lower), 13, 14, 15 (both).

Photographs of the following paintings appear by kind permission of the copyright holders: *Weeping Woman* by Pablo Picasso DACS 1992; and *Marilyn* by Andy Warhol. © 1992 The Andy Warhol Foundation for the Visual Arts/ARS, New York

Index